Sebastian Tidies Up

That's better!

Written by Mary-Anne Creasy
Illustrated by Alex Stitt

sundance

Sebastian was always tidying up
after everyone.

"It's a good thing that I'm here to look
after everybody," Sebastian said to
himself. "Otherwise no one would know
where anything was."

One day, when no one was
at home, Sebastian found
Dad's keys on the bookshelf.

3

"Dad will never remember that
he left his keys there," said Sebastian.
"I'll hang them on the hook beside the
telephone."

"Look at that. There are Mom's glasses. She can't read a thing without them. They could get scratched lying beside the telephone," said Sebastian. "I'll put them in this drawer."

5

He saw Grandma's
gardening gloves
in the drawer.

"These gloves belong
on the table by the door,"
said Sebastian.

6

On the table
by the door,
Sebastian found his
friend Isabella's
schoolbook.

"Lucky I saw this.
Isabella would
be in real
trouble if
she forgot
she left
it here!"

7

He put Isabella's book
safely on the bookshelf.
"That's much better,"
he said to himself,
as he raced off
to play basketball.

8

A little later, Isabella came over. Grandma and Mom were searching for their things.

"What will I do without my glasses?" asked Mom. "I can't read a thing without them."

"Where are my gardening gloves?" asked Grandma. "How can I work in the flower garden without my gloves?"

"Where's my book?" asked Isabella. "I have to take it to school tomorrow."

And then
Dad came in.
"I can't find my
keys anywhere,"
he said.

10

"Which keys?" asked Grandma.

"The keys to the car," said Dad.
"The keys to the office, the keys to everything! I can't find them anywhere!"

"I can't find my schoolbook,"
said Isabella.

"I can never find anything in this house,"
said Mom.

"Things never seem to stay where
I put them," said Grandma.

"Where did you leave your keys?"
asked Isabella.

"I thought I left them on the bookshelf,"
said Dad.

Isabella went over to the bookshelf.
"Look, there's my book. That's strange.
I'm sure I left it on the table by the door."

"There are my gloves," said Grandma.
"They are on that table by the door.
That's odd. I always leave them
in the drawer."

"There are my glasses," said Mom.
"How strange. I left them by
the telephone."

13

"There are my keys," said Dad. "How did they get there? I always leave them on the bookshelf. Everyone knows that!"

15

Later that afternoon, Sebastian
came home. He found Dad's keys
on the bookshelf.

"What a mess!" he said to himself.
"It's a good thing that I'm here to look
after everybody. Otherwise no one would
know where anything was."

16